seeds of sweetness

In loving memory of

FARON NICHOLS FARRELL

When Angels Paint The Town

Sally is writing this story as Faith
because Faith makes things happen
and brings lost souls together!
Bear in mind stories are not
Sally's style but she's doing
the best she can to write one here!
It needs to be told and it was requested,
hopefully you're not sorry
for the request..............

Twice Upon A Time
because Once Is Not Enough
for Their Love So Divine!
It was a good life for her but
something was missing.He on the other hand
was pretty much a loner till he met her and
the rest is history....
Faron got employed straight out of high school
at a local mill which became a steady job.
Although he had good enough
grades for college but it wasn't meant to be!
Sally got average grades
just enough to graduate cause she hated school.
She loafed a year then worked here and there
but nothing steady.She got hired at a local mill
in 1981 yes the same one as you know who!
She only worked there 4 months but got something
better than a job out of it!Their eyes met and
it was if nothing that happened before mattered.
She used to sit and wait
for him to come out at a table inside
the door to talk to him and he didn't mind at all!
They went to the mill christmas party and were
together ever since!
He nursed her through hardships that
later came along and hung in there when her nerves

and worrying got the better of her:it grew as she grew!
But he would patiently calm her fears.
She stuck by him through rough patches and together
they found heaven in their own little world!
They shared a bond as well as the same name:
the name Dear!But were known to others as
Faron And Sally:The Golden Couple like sunflowers
all year round!The townspeople couldn't help but
enjoy the beautiful picture:the light of Love
that stands the test of time!
Sadly they both lose their Fathers suddenly.Faron's Mother
became seriously ill and required constant care!
He being an only child caused friction
between Sally and her! Faron saw to it that His Mother
was taken care of while working full time.But he
Always found the time for Sally!Even if it meant
walking in snow storms when his car was plowed in etc.
just to be with her and do for her!
Sadly Faron's Mother then passed away.
And i can't forget the family cat that passed away!
Precious Faron w/tears in his eyes saying the cat died!
Never afraid to show emotion and love:that's
the measure of a real man in my book/story!
Sally's Mom later also became seriously ill and Sally
along with Faron saw to her every need till she
sadly passed away!That's how big
their hearts were and still are:
making their parents proud to this day!
For 29 years they cried then laughed,danced
and sang away the blues together!My Special Angel
became their song from the start!
Sally one day wrote a poem titled:And God Said.
Faron thought it was a masterpiece!Then soon after
the poetry just started to flow!Between their love
his inspiration and pride a poet was born!
November 28th of this year 2011 would have been
30 years of their heavenly bliss!But tragically
Faron passed away on March 11th 2011!
She tickled him 1 last time but he didn't quiver
that left her with the coldest never ending chill!
The house that once was Home
became just a house again....
where beautiful but painful memories live alone!
Suddenly nothing else that happens after mattered:
Sally's life on earth also ended but her love
for him lives on forever!

Of course she is a lost soul no matter how much
she believes in God and in Her Faith
not having Faron's physical being makes her lost!
But his love is always like a summer breeze
she can feel it gently tickling her in hopes that
it will wake her up to shine her light again!
Through eternity they will be
each others Special Angel spiritually!
And one fine day they will be reunited physically
because their love is meant to be!
It's rare to find this kind of love and nothing
can take it away!But only a reunion that Faith
will bring can give them both real Peace!!!!
Copyright Nov.14th 2011
Faith aka Sally

even the other sunflowers bowed to them....

~~1 satiny~~ comfort 2011 from heaven

When i was just a wee lass,
i had a comfort zone.
But it was not my blanket,
for my gikey was all my own.
I'd suck my thumb,
while rubbing the satin trim.
And say gike-gike-gike
away my blues went on a whim.
When i became a big lass,
still at times i felt blue.
I took comfort in knowing that,
with the love of my life beside me:
there's nothing i couldn't get thru.
Without him now to touch:
there's no comfort to cling to!
Copyright 2011
Sally

I Want You for the Sally Support Team

to dance with white cloud

It will be a year tomorrow
when i started on MY journey of sorrow,
i'm no further ahead than i was before
can't get past him laying alongside the road....
after greeting me seeming fine inside the door.
When i look past those last couple minutes
i see myself here with him where he sits,
but it's just a memory that hurts so much
cause a memory i can't physically touch.
I'll never accept what happened that day
i still think it's just a nightmare that'll go away,
watching and listening at the door for him
to continue OUR journey on earth shared in heaven.
Why didn't they bring him back to me
why'd they end on earth our life most heavenly,
why didn't i get the chance
to nurse him back to health so we could dance?
He held me close like a big fluffy white cloud
making me feel so safe and proud,
in his arms i couldn't help but float
on each other our hearts would dote.
Without him physically here i've lost my usefulness
but he should have woke up w/my tickle and kiss,
he felt them i know he did
but he should be here excited like....
Christmas Morning as a kid.
I'm waiting here Dear to give you your tickle
please please come back My Special Angel,
my fingers are numb from waiting it's so wrong
but they'll wake up when on you where they belong!
Copyright 2012
a year in the existence of many an endless tear....
Sally

a wish from faith

This is Faith wishing you lived closer
to Sally so you could hold her,
and tell her it'll be ok
even tho she wouldn't believe you anyway.
It would still be nice
if once or twice,
when her Mama3 gets too busy
she could depend on somebody.
Without Faron here she just wants to die
making Faith just want to cry,
Hope feels like there's just no way
that the memory of his earthly Love....
can get her thru the day.
She's not at a crossroad
she's just got too heavy a load,
she can't carry it being so weak and small
she falls short when expected to stand tall.
We both thank you for all your prayer
she needs all the help she can get to bear,
bear with all the sorrow
she doesn't even want to see tomorrow.
It's a front she puts up you think is brave
but her back against the wall....
only Faron can save,
it's a sad story but true
giving up's the best she can do.
If you read her truthful poem
you'll see how far she's fallen,
she can't get up she's fell too hard
she can't be healed....
she's too battered and scarred!
Copyright 2011
Faith holding onto Hope out of Love
aka S@L buried inside Sally
if only there was a trace of Goodolesal

Keep Faith With Me

As 1 person at least i believe
has come to know,
the metaphor that does weave
around my heart so!
My imagination is unending
My Precious Faron marveled at it,
it is my way to escape and keep on sending
appreciation to him while i lose....
my shattered self a bit!
Faith is not a person
but rather a feeling,
that i'll be with Faron
only then i'll be healing!
Bear w/me don't leave me please or be mad
i never lied and said Faith was a person you see,
but IF you thought so weren't you glad
when you thought she kept me company?
The truth is for the 1st time in my life....
nobody else is here
but Faith was and is my way,
of helping me thru the fear
that does visit me every single day!
I guess i kind of
tried to invent a friend,
because along w/me Faron My One True Love
know it won't but want my loneliness to end!
But another truth will remain
this computer screen i look to,
although to look at it may be plain
it comes to life when i see all of you!
Now when Faith comes to call
just keep in mind,
Faith Is with me thru it all
so i guess a Faithful Friend here i(did)find!
Faith comes along
Sally can disappear for awhile,
is it so wrong
to imagine i'm somebody else....
that unlike me has a reason to smile?
All the messages and every poem
came from Faith and My Heart,
i alone can't deal with the burden
that's where Faith plays a big part!
As for me(here) i'll never come to life again

it bears repeating i just exist,
when the pearly gates open up in heaven
i'll then be alive when by Faron i am kissed!
I truly am a lost soul
and need all the prayers+help i can get,
without him physically here My Special Angel
a sweet friend called death i can't forget!
If you really truly care
and know me you'll know i'd never lie,
it's just(i)alone all this can't bear
even with Faith endless tears i cry!
Copyright 2011
I try whatever way to reach out
isn't that what desperation's about?!
Not only that but Faith might be liked more
cause Faith's not a burden like i am for sure!!
Oh maybe just maybe if i pretend enuff
a real person may come keep me company+stuff!!
Sally

Hope And Faith

A monkey and a bird get lost and go into a bar....

All the people say
what good is that bird anyway,
she's only got 1 leg to stand on there
what if trouble is upon you somewhere?
Well the monkey says with such sincere eyes
how many among you gals and guys,
would just be there to hear
and listen to what brings the other fear?
Well nobody spoke up and the bird said so plain
my friend here Hope is her name,
she lost her mother one day
but she still stopped to help me along the way.
She's not completely herself anymore
but that's what hearts are for,
even tho on her own her troubles never end
she still had compassion to be my friend.
And my name is Faith if you have any interest
i lost the love of my life that once kissed,
kissed away my every pain
but the Faith in me knows....
he's still there watching over me thru the rain.
He lives in my heart i say it out loud
and i want him of me to stay proud,
so i try not to turn bitter and cold
till his wings again around me hold.
I'm there for Hope when she just wants to talk
and in my friendship she puts so much stock,
she's there for me even w/my wish to die so great
TRYING to make me see it's not yet my time....
for me to again fly with my soul mate!
Copyright 2011
Sally aka Faith

Goodnight Sleep Tight Don't Let Another Angel Bite

From childhood to adulthood
the story is the same,
i couldn't have had it more good
cause thru it all comfort came.
Goodnight Teddy
goodnight in your chair,
goodnight to me
because you're there.
You're cuddly and warm
good day to me when i'm cold,
thru any storm
you're with me to hold.
Goodnight Darkness
don't make me cry,
my teddy i'll kiss
so fears go bye bye.
When i'm big and grown
no more imaginary best friend that's the plan,
i'll still never be alone
Big Ole Teddy Bear Becomes My Man.
Goodnight Snuggle Bear Pooh
good holding you My Dear,
just having you
Heaven is here.
Sweet Dreams Angel
you make me complete,
My Heart And Soul
there's no better treat.
I must have been dreaming
cause when i did rise,
My All My Everything
not physically seen by my eyes.
Goodnight Chair
where you sat,
Goodnight In Heaven Up There
where my dream's at!
Copyright 2012
Now i'm back to an imaginary best friend
I'll have him again for real that true story has no end....
Sally

to hear the pitter patter of angel feet

When i got bored he'd say so cute
make some pictures....
write a poem do a tribute,
well Dear that's what i will do
and it's all for you.
Afterall you inspired me so
without that this gift i wouldn't know,
so this gift i send to heaven
but i cry so for you to....
see them here in person.
Every single day for me is hard My Love
so much you can't do with me from above,
i know your spirit is there....
for me to lean on
but your computer chair is empty....
where you sat upon.
Upon that chair you sang with me
when i played our songs so joyfully,
now i can't play music....
it's too hard to bear
without your beautiful voice....
chiming in there.
It doesn't matter what kind of song plays
i'm flooded with tears missing those days,
those days even when....
you sang a wrong word
the perfect voice of an angel i heard.
You always said you couldn't sing
well when you did my heart would ring,
ring out with happiness so true....
and so proud
i wanna sing with you again....
even in the rain i'm crying out loud.
But if you were here....
we'd sing in the sunshine
with you around....
all my days were that fine,
it's unbearable on earth anymore
without you My Precious....
coming thru the door.
Oh please come thru the door....
on your angel feet
that's the only way to make me complete,
i'm dying here heart and soul

what happens next i have no control.
I wanna play with you on your cloud
and get back my inner child,
i'm too weak now to be young at heart
tired and weary plays too big a part.
The months turn into years
the days fill up with tears,
tears i can not help but cry
cause time won't let me die.
To die in your arms i pray
will happen soon one day,
but i can't die in your arms....
heaven's where you bed down
and i can't die i'm already dead....
i just need planted in the ground.
From there i'll rise up from the dust
and then(lie)in your arms so just,
please Dear send me a sign
to let me know it'll soon be my time!
Copyright 2011
i keep waiting and waiting and waiting
Sally

precious moments etched in time,
an angel was here and all mine!

Mashed Potato Dream

Smothered in such thick gravy
dining on life so easy,
even with the lumps in the way
he could smooth them out any day.
2 peas from the pod each with a pearly onion
satisfied in our hunger for Heaven,
and corn on the cob so sweet
the cornier the better you can't beat.
Oh how i hunger got no ups all downs
without the sweet Hash in the country Browns,
golden brown to be precise
once upon a time should happen twice.
And then it happens by the Minute
i can smell that Rice from where i sit,
he never let remnants go to waste
he'd cook it up w/a nice finish to the taste.
And the chicken so country fried
you'd think you went to Heaven and died,
so many things not cooked anymore
those smells no longer escaping out the door.
I get to where i don't have the heart
to eat certain things cause he's not here to take part,
he taught me about mashed potatoes with corn
never before heard of that since i was born.
I only eat cause i have to
to not that kind of sick i don't have to do,
but still all in all now i rarely cook
but i dream of when i did he'd come runnin to look!
Copyright 2012
Sweet Taters McFrenzie Sally

go tender into the world

A fragile butterfly
and a mighty wolf met one day.
The butterfly being so tiny
and the wolf so big and tall
there was still no fear.
For this was not your typical wolf.
It carried the butterfly on its back
whenever it was in pain and couldn't fly.
Even though mighty its tender side
was so strong and rare among its kind.
They kept pretty much to themselves
most of the time because it was safe.
But were gentle and kind to others
that crossed their path.
They huddled together in the cold
and in the warm they took in all
the beauty of the land.
They were more content just being together.
The wolf would go out for food
and they drank water from the stream.
The butterfly's wings were so soft
against the wolf's body and it
was calming when the wolf got upset or tired.
The butterfly would fly about
making music with its wings and
the wolf would howl in delight.
Oh they were so happy and complete.
Until sadly one day the wolf collapsed
and went to sleep. And although the butterfly
had wings being too weak from grief
it just stayed to itself
waiting for the wind to carry it away
to a better peaceful place.
The wolf now howls at the moon
in pain from missing its soulmate.
And even though their time on earth is over
i truly believe they'll meet again
because a bond like that nothing can take destroy!
Copyright 2012

always a watchful eye said the wolf to the butterfly....
Sally

a late bloomer outblooms the rest

Too short but true story
about the magnetism
we had from the start.
He's a chick magnet alright
AND THAT CHICK IS ME!
Sift thru the words if you will
and let them soak in.
This is how my life/my living began
and it all started with
MY precious 1 of a kind man....

He was 26 yrs.old never had
a serious encounter already in adulthood.
I was 24 and had sifted thru
my share of garbage along the way.
I gave him special treatment
and he quickly ate that up.
Our eyes met and he sensed my interest.
I sensed his awe as a child
on christmas morning.
We both enjoyed the fruit
of our labor of love the apple,
and in this case not forbidden.
In many weak moments....
i'm in need of peace
that lacks within,
it is his awe that i will seek.
A common path we walked together
for with his feeling of awe in my soul
what will i lack?
I know i won't lack
the ability to appreciate....
what's important in life and that is love.
Our love never got old it was always new,
and when it's love like that
it will stand the test of time and tragedy!
Copyright 2011
CERTAINLY NOT-THE END
Sally

to kill a mynah bird

She was small but was spirited.
She didn't like to be caged
so she would break out and explore.
Afraid to be herself though
she would mimic the other female birds.
Many male birds liked her company
and she got the feeling she could fit in.
Years went by and she
felt like 1 of the birds
but still hungered for more.
One day along came a bird
of a different feather.
He said he sensed something special
and that she wasn't being herself.
She then felt her spirit come alive
 and that she could soar higher
than the rest and to
get the flock out of there.
The others were holding her back
and she finally found her sanctuary.
Together they built a love nest
and she found her own voice as well.
She started to mimic the song in her heart
and he happily would sing along.
One day he sadly stopped singing
and just went to sleep.
She was silenced from then on
and just stayed in the nest all alone.
She folded her wings over her breast
waiting to go to sleep herself!
Copyright 2012
no more happy voice and not by choice
Sally

Limericks Seriously

These limericks take a different turn
they're very serious this time
i truly hope you learn
to treasure true love so fine....

There was a woman from pennsylvania
her troubles will truly drain ya
she's sorry to burden you all
only on true friends she'll call
cause life can be cold like siberia.

There once were 2 peas in a pod him and me
growing in warmth for all to see
then one day came such a cold snap
now i just wanna take a dirt nap
cause that pod can't survive with just 1 pea.

There was a woman who treasured her lil'blue box
where she's had so many comforting talks
if she were to die tomorrow
you'll miss her with such sorrow
but she'll spread sunshine when trouble knocks.

There once was a couple so happy
who lived life so snappy
then tragically one day
life just up and took their zest away
but it can't take their memory.

Copyright 2012
Sally

tuck in tinymite heaven tonite

I AM SO LONELY
I NEED MY SWEETIE
TO COME HOLD ME
THIS HAPPENING CAN'T BE!!!!
I see him when
my eyes are closed or open,
but when i reach out for him
it's just air empty within!!!!
I can't do this i swear
i keep seeing him here and there,
but something cold's always in the air
it's endless chills of pain i can't bear!!!!
I'll go to sleep
deep purple dream creep,
i'll no longer weep
sweet peace i'll keep!!!!
I MAY BE TINY
BUT MY NEED MIGHTY
SOON I GO NIGHTY
ALL RIGHTY AND TIGHTY!!!!
Copyright 2011
Sally

Be Gone Blue Moon:The Awakening

Good Grief Angel White
there is so much bad day and night,
nothing good can come of
me here and you up above.
There is never any good to grief
even reaching out no relief,
every single day gets worse
when not(picked up)by the hearse.
Each time that i rise
i can't look into your hazel green eyes,
thru them such beauty was seen
now only darkness in-between.
In-between my world each corner
there is no light of day ever,
only when i join you will i see
the light which on earth went out for me.
I'll go to sleep to a blue moon mistake
till it turns gold don't let me wake,
i'll have no peace or no glow till i lie
in the arms of my treasured guy!
Copyright 2012
Sally

a valentine story haiku

I proudly love him
yes every day of my life
not just sweethearts day

Though sweethearts day is
the best time to show your love
show it every day

Like a butterfly
beauty with love oh so rare
delicate yet strong

No doubt come one day
loved ones sadly leave this earth
treasure each moment

Precious moments shared
down memory lane over tea
someone there for tears

Never be afraid
to give someone all of you
the returns priceless

If you're not loved back
by loving you did your best
at least you did try

I'm thankful i had
my place in the sun with him
now i have sweet dreams

(each 1 stands alone but also tells a story)
Copyright 2012
Sally

a valentine tickle and then some angel

Valentines Day a week from tomorrow
mine will be filled w/memories and sorrow,
sorrow that here My Precious won't be anymore
and his sweet presence+kiss but memories by the score.
Oh how i miss the cards w/his sweet poem
can't bear to think there'll be no more from him,
but here every single day was valentines day
giving each other sweets always came into play.
From a tickle to a song
we quivered and sang all the day long,
and tho candy is dandy
twas never as sweet as the pleasure he gave me.
Faron i miss you more each day My Dear
not a day goes by without many a tear,
nor does any day ever end
without my heart breaking that only your kiss can mend.
Hold Me Squeeze Me Please Me:Come Back Home
Your Pooh is still in here all alone,
1 day soon i won't wake up here anymore My Sweet
i'll meet you up there and even tickle your feet!
(that's a promise My Angel you can take to the moon- heart)
Copyright 2012
Sally

The Last Of The Glow Beacons

My Mother told me there'd be days of sweet bliss
but she never said i'd spend years without His Kiss,
and she said the right 1 i'd find out....
all the time was in my back yard
but she never said i'd be so young+alone w/a life so hard.
This loving woman so beautiful
was filled with so much wisdom heart and soul,
she taught me to treasure every second for sure
but she could never teach me how to stop watching the door.
For now the right 1 has been taken so tragically
i don't even have My Mommy to hold me,
with Faron not here the last of my close family on earth
i'm nothing alone i have no worth.
Mommy why did my world stop spinning around
why is there no laughter or sunshine found,
how can i go on without Him physically here
when will Peace and Mercy appear?
Precious Faron was there when i lost you
and comforted me like True Love should do,
sitting up with me and holding my hand
why isn't He here beside me now i don't understand?!
Him being on earth gave me reason to glow
a beacon of light that i'd proudly show,
now my light is out not just dim
cause i get no more warm kisses from him!
Copyright 2012
Even My Gikey Now Is No Use To Me
For No Good Can It Be Without Added Security....
Sally

the memory of my last christmas card

Suitably so he picked the card
THE* PAINTER* OF* LIGHT*
to help get me thru the night
****
****
****
****
****
****
****

(Every)card i got from him
had a sweet"personal"poem,
but this 1 i must share
cause of the tender loving care.
The care that was given so much
and that he'll never again touch,
touch his sweet poem on my card
to make hallmark eat their out....
for him that was not at all hard!
The message this card conveys
thru all of my days,
is that my angel will still be
there to comfort me!
Forgive me as i type this
if certain letters i miss,
sobbing uncontrolably is torture
on the heart of the writer!
I saved all of them since we began
began our journey as woman and man,
that we traveled thru undying love
blessed by....
The Sweetest Angel From Above!
Copyright 2011
Sally

Just remember an angel(to me) wrote this
and sealed it with a kiss....

Christmas comes but once a year
and it goes so fast

I hope this card will bring you joy
and make your holidays last

But if the joy of holidays
is once again gone&brings you fear

Just remember one small thing
i will still be here

May all your holidays be merry&bright

Love You,Always
Faron

Reading his poem makes me bluest of blue,
do you suppose the most precious of precious knew?

   {   AN ANGEL WAS HERE   }
and is staying-have no fear!

My heart 4ever true and sweet,
it can't miss w/an angel on the beat!

the angel whisperer

No i will not heal in this lifetime
days go by there's more despair,
cause my partner in living and rhyme
can't hold me when life isn't fair.
Tho i see him everywhere i go
it's just a painful reminder,
that his special touch i need so
in this life will not occur.
I'm terrified of all things now
even the quiet i once enjoyed,
the only thing that makes me smile
is knowing heaven awaits to fill the void.
Hopefully the promised land
will soon be welcoming me,
with my true love i'll walk hand in hand
where i'm meant to be.
My special angel will say my name again
in a whisper so very sweet,
but only when i get to heaven
w/magic my heart'll have rhythmic beat!
Copyright 2011
Sally

the angel wore football cleats

I never thought i'd miss football
it never turned me on,
but i'll miss his whooping call
i now wanna learn to play it....
on the clouds he floats upon.
It would be the most super
of all super bowls....
if he'd come home to see,
i'd throw him a pass....
for a touchdown 4ever
if he'd just come running back to me.
If there's football in Heaven
i hope he gets to watch....
and maybe play a game,
his uniform would read Pooh 1 for Faron
and football would never be the same.
My angel would trade in his halo
for a helmet of pure gold,
must protect that sweet head you know
where that smile shines so bright+bold.
Maybe this year
his team'll score 1 for the big dipper,
and from his stars he'll send me a cheer
that would make me feel chipper!
Copyright 2012
Fantasy Football i can get into
The Best Team Me And My Pooh
(with Faith as
our Coach
we'll play
2gether an eternity)
Sally

And the award goes to Faron for being such a sport to me. *ever cheering you on my favorite MVP XXOO~sally~

the law firm of angel gates

I truly have no life left now
and surrender what's left to thee,
my heart it stands on trial
Faron is my power of attorney.
My last will and testament
is to lie in his arms,
for here on earth i am spent
no protection from what harms.
For love is the law of the land
and without it to hold it's a crime,
he holds my fate / destiny in his hand
and for my case i'm not charged a dime.
The point of light
i pray soon will come,
i'll see it in his angelic eyes so bright
until then i'm legally blind and numb.
Copyright 2011
Sally

a message wrapped in fur

This poem will be short and sweet
a message delivered by 4 little feet,
it made me cry but so cute to behold
i just thought it had to be told.
To think something of fur....
having such a tale
but it was there without fail,
it was a cotton of a tale so little but proud
just like it fell from my angel's cloud.
The other day a baby bunny
came by to visit me,
it's possible it was as if to say
our new life 2gether soon be underway.
It was so cute+little but it could run
maybe letting me know....
it won't be long till i'll be having fun,
fun w/my somebunny dear i'll 4ever love
before too long we'll run and play above.
Copyright 2011
Sally

Outside my porch grows
the weeping tree,
as everyone around knows
it has become close to me.
As i stand there
beneath it i feel now,
all the pain i can't bear
it shelters me somehow.
With each blossom
so sweet and pure,
i feel closer to Faron
like i'm standing....
Neath Heaven's Door!
(and a lil friend came by hoppily)

www.ingramcontent.com/pod-product-compliance
Lightning Source LLC
Chambersburg PA
CBHW041547220426
43665CB00002B/53